Wizard of Oz Activity Book

Pat Stewart

DOVER PUBLICATIONS, INC.
Mineola, New York

Copyright

Text copyright © 1999 by Dover Publications, Inc.
Illustrations copyright © 1999 by Pat Stewart
All rights reserved under Pan American and International Copyright Conventions.

Published in Canada by General Publishing Company, Ltd., 30 Lesmill Road, Don Mills, Toronto, Ontario.

Bibliographical Note

Little Wizard of Oz Activity Book is a new work, first published by Dover Publications, Inc., in 1999.

International Standard Book Number: 0-486-40735-7

Manufactured in the United States of America
Dover Publications, Inc., 31 East 2nd Street, Mineola, N.Y. 11501

Note

Relive the excitement of the *Wonderful Wizard of Oz* as you solve the challenging brainteasers and word searches in this little book. When you complete the puzzles, or if you get stuck, you'll find the solutions beginning on page 54. And don't forget, it's fun to color the pictures, too!

When Dorothy's house was caught in the cyclone, she lost Toto, her basket, her sunbonnet, a chair, a book, a bowl, and a pot.

Find and circle them in the picture above.

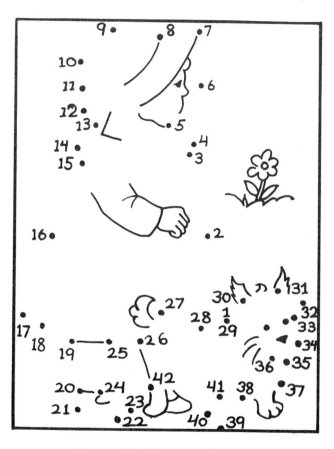

Connect the dots to see the picture.

These are the first people Dorothy met when she and Toto landed in Oz. Can you unscramble their name?

Dorothy got these silver shoes from
the Wicked Witch of the East.

Circle the correct pair in the picture above.

There were 4 witches in the Land of Oz.

① **WICKED WITCH OF THE EAST** (SHE HAS THE MAGIC SLIPPERS)

② **WICKED WITCH OF THE WEST** (SHE WEARS A PATCH)

③ **GOOD WITCH OF THE NORTH** (SHE HAS A MAGIC STAFF)

④ **GLINDA THE GOOD WITCH OF THE SOUTH** (SHE WEARS A CROWN)

Put the number of the correct name in the circle next to each witch.

Glinda the Good Witch has 2 beautiful crowns exactly alike.

Circle the 2 matching crowns in the picture above.

Circle the 8 things on the facing page which are different from the things on this page.

Dorothy and Toto are anxious to reach the Emerald City. Please help!

Dorothy is trying to help the Scarecrow in the middle of the cornfield. Can you find a clear path?

How many crows do you count in the picture above?
Write the number here. ____

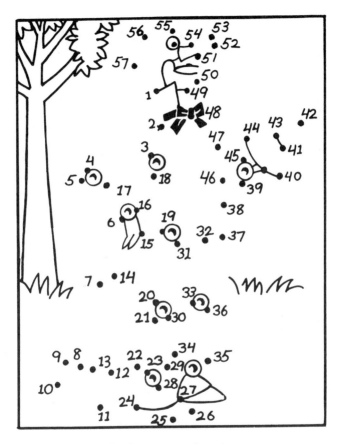

Connect the dots to complete the picture.

The Tin Woodman is looking for his hat, his axe, and the Scarecrow's hat. Find and circle them.

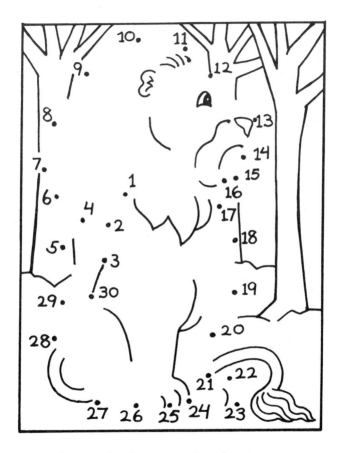

Connect the dots to complete the picture.

The Scarecrow needs to get Dorothy out of the poppy bed. Help him find the way.

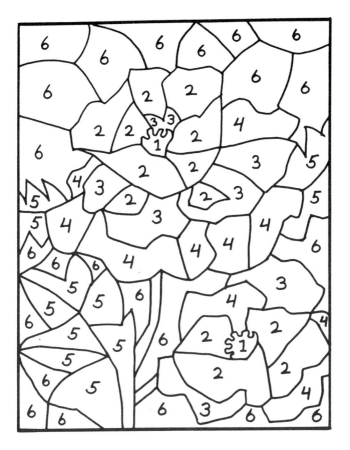

To see the picture, color in the spaces like this:
1=black; 2=pink; 3=red; 4=maroon;
5=green; 6=light blue.

Because the poor Lion can't wake up, the field mice are going to rescue him.

Find and circle the 8 mice hiding on this page.

Circle 11 things in this picture that are different in the picture on the opposite page.

What did Dorothy, the Scarecrow, the Tin Woodman, and the Lion want from the Wizard?

Put the number of the correct answer in the circle next to each character.

What did the Wizard of Oz want Dorothy to do?
Unscramble the words to find out.

Circle the pictures on this page whose names begin with the letter W.

Toto is playing with some friendly dogs.
Can you pick him out of the crowd?

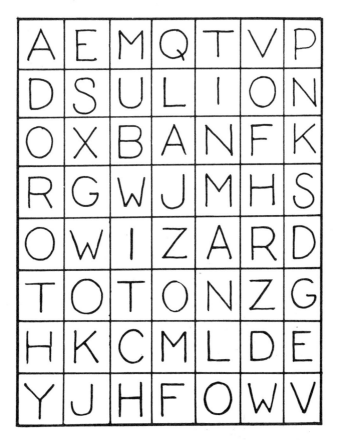

The words WITCH, WIZARD, DOROTHY, TOTO, TINMAN, and LION are hidden in the puzzle above. Find and circle them.

Dorothy and her friends are having dinner.
Circle the animals that don't belong.

Find and circle the names of these objects which are hidden in the puzzle on the facing page.

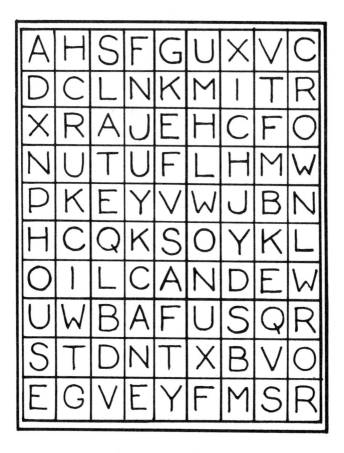

These are some of the people Dorothy met on her travels. Find and circle their names in the puzzle on the facing page.

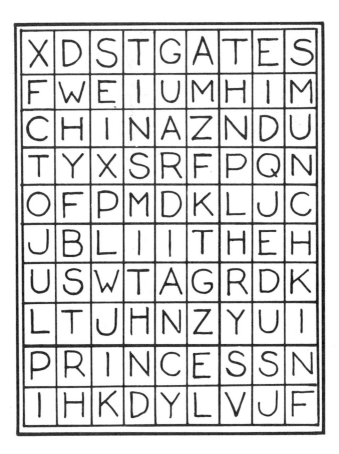

These are some of the odd creatures Dorothy met
on her travels. Find and circle their names
in the puzzle on the facing page.

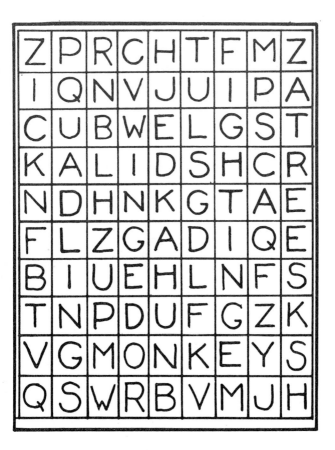

The poor Scarecrow is stuck on a pole in the river.
Three large birds have come to rescue him.

Put the number in the circle which correctly matches the bird and its name. 1=pelican; 2=eagle; 3=stork.

How did Dorothy destroy the Wicked Witch?
Unscramble the words to find out.

Dorothy used the charm of the Golden Cap
to call the Winged Monkeys. How many came?
Put the answer here.___

Unscramble the letters to make words that match the pictures.

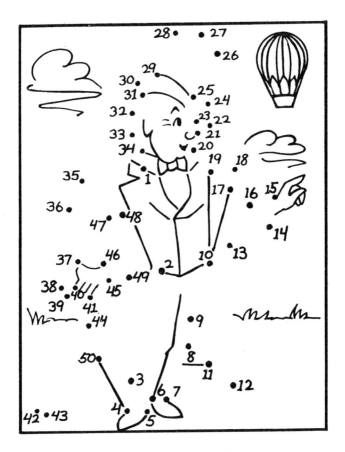

Connect the dots to find out who this is.

47

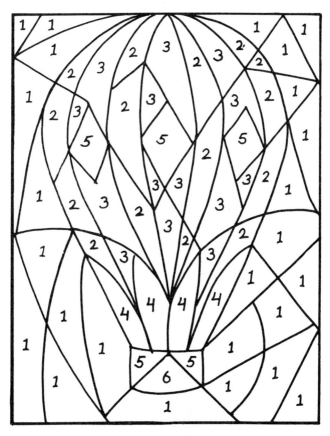

See the hidden picture when you color
in the numbered spaces like this: 1=light blue;
2=yellow; 3=orange; 4=lime green; 4=red; 6=maroon.

Dorothy wants to go home to Kansas.
Please help her find the way.

Dorothy is saying good-bye to her friends.
Unscramble the words to find out where she's going.

KACB HMEO OT NKSAAS

After Dorothy left Oz, the Lion, the Scarecrow, and the Tin Woodman each became king of his own country. Match the kingdoms and characters by writing the

correct numbers in the circles: 1=The Forest; 2=Oz and the Emerald City; 3=The Land of the Winkies.

Solutions

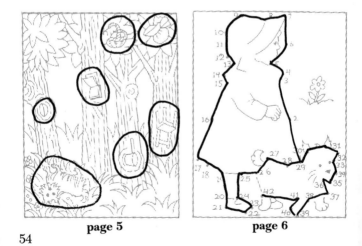

page 5   page 6

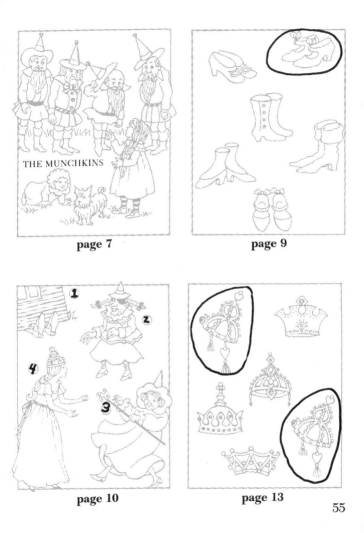

page 15

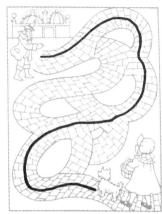
page 16

page 17

page 18

page 19

page 20

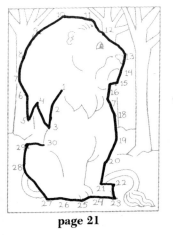
page 21

page 22

57

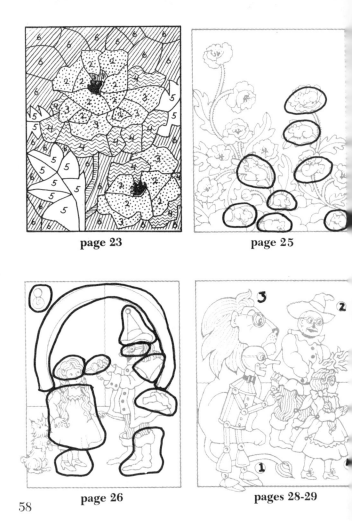

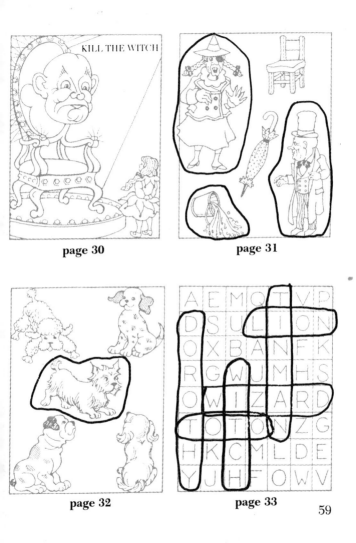

pages 34-35

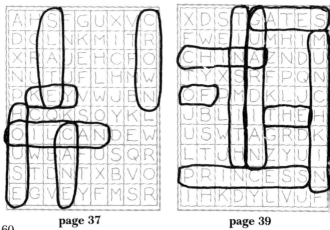

page 37

page 39

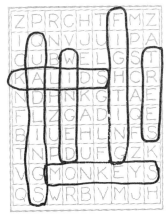

page 41

pages 42-43

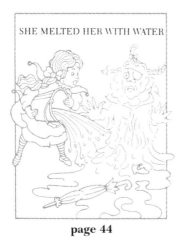

page 44

page 45

page 46

page 47

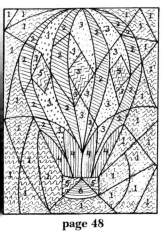

page 48

page 49

BACK HOME TO KANSAS

page 51

pages 52–53